W9-AGL-931

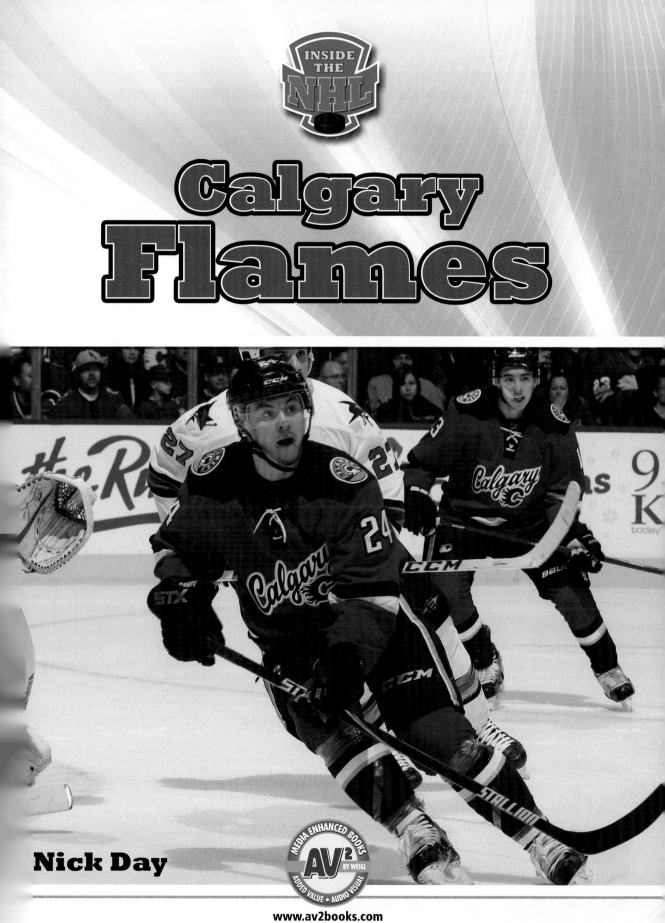

INSIDE THE NHL

Calgary Flames

Nick Day

AV2
MEDIA ENHANCED BOOKS
BY WEIGL
ADDED VALUE • AUDIO VISUAL

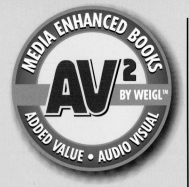

AV² provides enriched content that supplements and complements this book. Weigl's AV² books strive to create inspired learning and engage young minds in a total learning experience.

Your AV² Media Enhanced books come alive with...

Audio
Listen to sections of the book read aloud.

Key Words
Study vocabulary, and complete a matching word activity.

Video
Watch informative video clips.

Quizzes
Test your knowledge.

Go to **www.av2books.com**, and enter this book's unique code.

BOOK CODE

G 8 5 6 7 3 2

Embedded Weblinks
Gain additional information for research.

Slide Show
View images and captions, and prepare a presentation.

AV² by Weigl brings you media enhanced books that support active learning.

Try This!
Complete activities and hands-on experiments.

... and much, much more!

Published by AV² by Weigl
350 5th Avenue, 59th Floor
New York, NY 10118
Websites: www.av2books.com   www.weigl.com

Library of Congress Control Number: 2014951933

ISBN 978-1-4896-3119-0 (hardcover)
ISBN 978-1-4896-4014-7 (softcover)
ISBN 978-1-4896-3120-6 (single-user eBook)
ISBN 978-1-4896-3121-3 (multi-user eBook)

Printed in the United States of America in Brainerd, Minnesota
1 2 3 4 5 6 7 8 9 0   19 18 17 16 15

032015
WEP050315

Senior Editor Heather Kissock
Art Director Terry Paulhus

Photo Credits
Every reasonable effort has been made to trace ownership and to obtain permission to reprint copyright material. The publishers would be pleased to have any errors or omissions brought to their attention so that they may be corrected in subsequent printings.

Weigl acknowledges Getty Images and iStock as its primary image suppliers for this title.

CONTENTS

AV² Book Code. 2
Introduction 4
History 6
The Arena. 8
Where They Play 10
The Uniforms 12
Helmets and Face Masks 14
The Coaches 16
Fans and the Internet. 18
Legends of the Past 20
Stars of Today. 22
All-Time Records 24
Timeline 26
Write a Biography 28
Trivia Time 30
Key Words/Index 31
www.av2books.com. 32

Introduction

Hockey finally arrived in the city of Calgary, Alberta, Canada, in time for the 1980 National Hockey League (NHL) season, and the local fans could not have been more overjoyed. The bankrupt Atlanta Flames were looking for a new home under more stable ownership, and Calgary seemed to be the ideal destination. For years, the people of Calgary had watched with envy as Edmonton, the other major city in Alberta, rallied around its beloved Oilers. Finally, Calgary, a small industrial city, got in on the NHL action.

The Flames is hoping its crop of young players, including Johnny Gaudreau, will bring new energy to the team.

For the 34 seasons since the Flames' arrival, the people of Calgary have supported their dynamic team. The Flames have enjoyed periods of true dominance in their division—which is now called the Pacific Division—especially during the second half of the 1980s. Although the Flames' only Stanley Cup Championship win came in 1989, the fans' love of their local team has not subsided.

 The Flames last appeared in the Stanley Cup Final in 2004. They fell one win short of hoisting the Cup before being eliminated by the Tampa Bay Lightning in game seven.

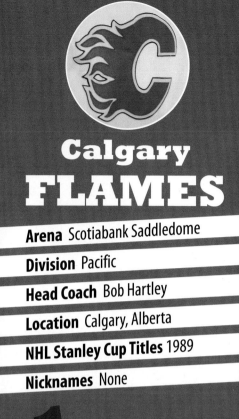

Calgary FLAMES

Arena Scotiabank Saddledome

Division Pacific

Head Coach Bob Hartley

Location Calgary, Alberta

NHL Stanley Cup Titles 1989

Nicknames None

1 Stanley Cup Title

6 Division Championships

9 Hall of Famers

20 Postseason Appearances

History

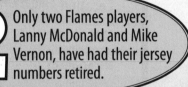

2 Only two Flames players, Lanny McDonald and Mike Vernon, have had their jersey numbers retired.

🦫 Mike Vernon played 13 seasons with the Flames, saving more than 12,000 shots on goal.

The Calgary Flames began play in the 1980 season when the Atlanta Flames moved to Calgary. The team was originally named for a famous Atlanta fire that destroyed much of the city near the end of the American Civil War. When the organization moved to Calgary, fans voted to keep the name intact, as a way of honoring Calgary's strong oil industry.

Upon arriving in "Cowtown," as Calgary is affectionately called, the Flames immediately created a winning tradition. Their first arena, the Stampede Corral, housed the Flames' first three successful seasons. Six years after moving to their second home, the Flames captured their first Stanley Cup title.

Fans were hooked immediately, as they had been craving an NHL team for years. It only took the Flames eight seasons in Calgary to capture a Stanley Cup title, which solidified the team's place as a major hockey power in both western Canada and the NHL. Further, it solidified the Flames as an integral part of the Calgary community.

The 2014–2015 season will mark Mark Giordano's second season as the Flames captain.

The Arena

Fans are treated to real flames during home games at the Scotiabank Saddledome in Calgary.

The Scotiabank Saddledome opened in the autumn of 1983 as the new home of the Calgary Flames. The arena also was built with a second purpose in mind—as the host hockey arena for the 1988 Winter Olympics. This meant that the Saddledome, which was originally called Olympic Saddledome, was designed to be a true world-class hockey venue. The Flames, and their fans, were thrilled to call it their home.

The Saddledome got its name because the roof of the building is U-shaped, much like a saddle. The roof is turned up at the ends and sags in the middle. This feature immediately sets the arena apart, distinguishing the dome as unique among other sports venues. Top to bottom, the Saddledome is also quite intimate. Although there are three tiers of seating, the farthest sightline in the arena, from seat to the ice floor, is only 200 feet (61 meters).

German figure skater Katarina Witt won her second gold medal at the Saddledome in 1988. She was the first figure skater to win two Olympic gold medals.

Where They Play

CANADA

British Columbia — 7

Alberta — 4

Scotiabank Saddledome, Calgary — ★3

Saskatchewan

Manitoba — 14

Ontario

Washington

Montana

North Dakota

Minnesota — 11

Wisconsin — 8

Oregon

Idaho

South Dakota

Iowa

Illinois

UNITED STATES

Nevada — 6

Utah

Wyoming

Nebraska

California

Colorado — 9

Kansas

Missouri — 13

5

1

Arizona — 2

New Mexico

Oklahoma

Arkansas

Pacific Ocean

Texas — 10

Louisiana

MEXICO

Gulf of Mexico

NHL WESTERN CONFERENCE

PACIFIC DIVISION
1 Anaheim Ducks
2 Arizona Coyotes
★3 Calgary Flames
4 Edmonton Oilers
5 Los Angeles Kings
6 San Jose Sharks
7 Vancouver Canucks

CENTRAL DIVISION
8 Chicago Blackhawks
9 Colorado Avalanche
10 Dallas Stars
11 Minnesota Wild
12 Nashville Predators
13 St. Louis Blues
14 Winnipeg Jets

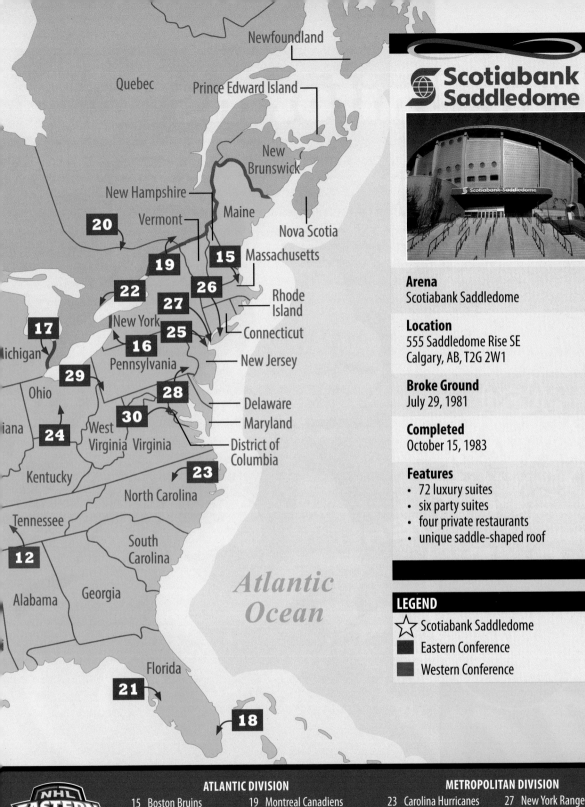

Scotiabank Saddledome

Arena
Scotiabank Saddledome

Location
555 Saddledome Rise SE
Calgary, AB, T2G 2W1

Broke Ground
July 29, 1981

Completed
October 15, 1983

Features
- 72 luxury suites
- six party suites
- four private restaurants
- unique saddle-shaped roof

LEGEND
☆ Scotiabank Saddledome
■ Eastern Conference
■ Western Conference

NHL EASTERN CONFERENCE

ATLANTIC DIVISION

15 Boston Bruins
16 Buffalo Sabres
17 Detroit Red Wings
18 Florida Panthers
19 Montreal Canadiens
20 Ottawa Senators
21 Tampa Bay Lightning
22 Toronto Maple Leafs

METROPOLITAN DIVISION

23 Carolina Hurricanes
24 Columbus Blue Jackets
25 New Jersey Devils
26 New York Islanders
27 New York Rangers
28 Philadelphia Flyers
29 Pittsburgh Penguins
30 Washington Capitals

The Uniforms

When the Calgary Flames debuted in 1980, the team's jerseys were the highest-selling jerseys in all of sports.

The Flames have only had **ONE** alternative design in team history. The flaming horse head appeared on alternate and away jerseys at various times from 1998 through 2006.

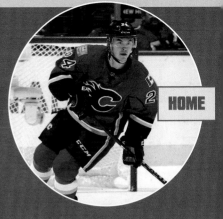

HOME

In the Flames' 34 seasons in Calgary, the team's uniforms have not undergone many changes. The current design features either red or white jerseys, depending on whether the team is home or away, with the Flames **logo** on the front of the jersey. The Flames logo is a red or black "C," surrounded by flames.

AWAY

In the early 2000s, the team tried to popularize an alternative logo, with the face of a horse surrounded by flames. That logo was not popular with the fans and has since faded. The team has returned to its classic flaming "C" logo. An alternative jersey, one with "Calgary" written out in black script, was recently introduced and has been well received in Calgary.

The Flames have worn many different combinations of the team's four primary colors of red, yellow, black, and white on their jerseys.

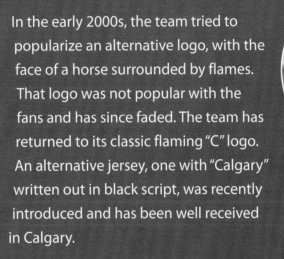

Helmets and Face Masks

Flames players wear their jersey numbers on their helmets.

he Flames wear helmets that match the uniforms they wear on game days. At home, they generally wear black helmets and red uniforms. The sides of the helmets read "Calgary," written out in red and yellow script. Flames goalies have a long tradition of designing their own face masks, as most goalies do. Historically, Flames goalies have used the team logo, covering their helmets in frightening flames that spread from the goalie's face mask and cover most of the helmet.

Flames players and fans also have an interesting tradition involving firefighter helmets. There is a strong partnership between the Flames and the Calgary Fire Department, which gave rise to the tradition in the first place. The Flames organization owns one stylish firefighter's helmet covered in flames, which is given to the hardest-working Flames player after every game. In the locker room, Flames players celebrate the recipient of the special helmet.

Flames goalies use various images of fire on their helmets. These red-hot designs display team colors and pride.

The Coaches

193 Bob Johnson leads all Flames coaches, with 193 wins.

Bob Hartley is well-known as one of the more demanding coaches in the NHL. He often gets very animated in conversations with players during games.

The Calgary Flames have had 16 different coaches in **franchise** history, and three of them were brothers with the same last name, Sutter. Although the 1989 Stanley Cup marked the team's crowning achievement, there has not been a shortage of victories and winning seasons in Calgary. In fact, nine of the 14 coaches who left Calgary did so with a winning record.

TERRY CRISP Terry Crisp became coach of the Flames in the 1987 season, and helped the organization continue on its path toward hockey's highest prize. His high point in Calgary was leading the team to its only Stanley Cup Championship victory in 1989.

DARRYL SUTTER Darryl Sutter has brought success to every NHL team he has coached, and the Flames are no exception. Sutter directed Calgary to the Stanley Cup Final in 2004, and during his three seasons as head coach, compiled a 107-73-15 record. He joined the team in 2002–2003 and left in 2006.

BOB HARTLEY Bob Hartley is the current coach of the Calgary Flames, moving behind the bench in 2012. Hartley has a distinguished NHL coaching pedigree, including a 2001 Stanley Cup victory as the head man for the Colorado Avalanche. Hartley is respected throughout the NHL, and fans in Calgary have entrusted their Stanley Cup aspirations to him.

Fans and the Internet

The Flames averaged 19,302 spectators at home games during the 2013–2014 season, good for the seventh-highest attendance in the NHL.

When they are not in their seats at the Saddledome, Flames fans can often be found on forums such as Calgarypuck, www.calgarypuck.com, as well as Matchsticks and Gasoline, matchsticksandgasoline.com. These are both unofficial fan websites run by die-hard members of the Flames community. The sites feature news, analysis, and discussion boards where fans can celebrate the team's successes and vent their frustrations during losing streaks.

The Flames are also very involved in the Calgary community. One community tradition is the annual Wheelchair Hockey Challenge, in which Flames players play wheelchair floor hockey against the Townsend Tigers, a team of young hockey fans who are in wheelchairs because of disabilities. The Tigers have beaten the Flames every year since 1981.

Signs
of a fan

 Flames fans, especially in **playoff games**, are often dressed head to toe in the Flames' iconic bright red. Together they are called "The 'C' of Red."

 Flames fans love celebrating a Calgary goal or win with Monster Truck's "Righteous Smoke" blaring from the Saddledome sound system.

Legends of the Past

Many great players have suited up for the Flames. A few of them have become icons of the team and the city it represents.

Lanny McDonald

Lanny McDonald had a storied NHL career that began in Toronto and ended in Calgary, with the Flames. McDonald, a high-scoring forward, joined the Flames in just their second season in Calgary. McDonald quickly won over the fans with his fast-paced and efficient style. In his best season with the Flames, McDonald recorded 66 goals and 32 **assists** in 80 games. Calgary reached the playoffs every year that he played for the Flames. In the 1986 postseason, when the Flames went to their first Stanley Cup Final, McDonald recorded 11 goals.

Position: Right Wing
NHL Seasons: 16 (1973–1989)
Born: February 16, 1953, in Hanna, Alberta, Canada

Jarome Iginla

Jarome Iginla played for the Flames from 1996 to 2013. Still an active player in the NHL, Iginla spent his best years in the league as part of the Flames. During his 16 complete seasons in Calgary, Iginla was a scoring machine, putting up multiple 30-goal seasons, and two seasons with 50 or more goals. Iginla is the all-time Flames leader in almost every category, including games played, goals, and shots. He is remembered fondly by Calgary fans.

Position: Right Wing
NHL Seasons: 18 (1996–Present)
Born: July 1, 1977, in Edmonton, Alberta, Canada

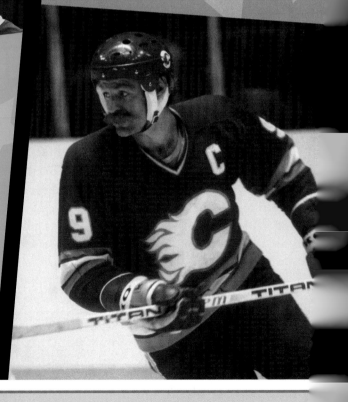

Mike Vernon

Mike Vernon is fondly remembered as one of the most legendary goalies to ever wear the Flames' red jersey. A hometown boy, born and raised in Calgary, Vernon was thrilled to join the team's ranks in 1982. Vernon quickly became a fixture between the pipes in Calgary, and was instrumental in the Flames' quick rise to consistent success. During his many seasons with the Flames, Vernon recorded a yearly **save percentage** of 88.3, putting him among the elite goaltenders in the NHL.

Position: Goalie
NHL Seasons: 20
(1982–2002)
Born: February 24, 1963, in Calgary, Alberta, Canada

Al MacInnis

Al MacInnis was one of the original Calgary Flames, joining the team in its second season in Canada. MacInnis was a valuable asset to the Flames, quickly becoming a reliable and popular player. Despite a few serious injuries, MacInnis was as consistent on both ends of the rink as any defenseman in the league. MacInnis regularly eclipsed the 50-assists mark, an impressive statistic for a defenseman. He was well known for having one of the hardest shots in the NHL.

Position: Defenseman
NHL Seasons: 23 (1981–2004)
Born: July 11, 1963, in Inverness, Nova Scotia, Canada

Stars of Today

Today's Flames team is made up of many young, talented players who have proven that they are among the best in the league.

Mark Giordano

Mark Giordano is the current team captain for the Flames. Giordano took over the post of captain from the legendary Jarome Iginla, who held the honor from 2003 to 2013. Giordano has played nine seasons in Calgary, and has become a fixture in red and white. Giordano has established himself as an intense, relentless player with some offensive prowess. Giordano scores more goals than the typical defenseman, making him a threat on both ends of the ice. In the 2010–2011 season, Giordano led Flames defensemen in scoring with eight goals and 43 total points.

Position: Defenseman
NHL Seasons: 9 (2005–Present)
Born: October 3, 1983, in Toronto, Ontario, Canada

Sean Monahan

Position: Center
NHL Seasons: 2 (2013–Present)
Born: October 12, 1994, in Brampton, Ontario, Canada

Sean Monahan was chosen by the Flames in the first round of the 2013 NHL **Entry Draft**. Since Monahan was only 19 when he debuted with the Flames, he was eligible to return to the junior leagues. However, Monahan declared he was ready to play in the NHL, and he became the first junior-eligible player to make the jump to the Flames roster in 33 years. Monahan immediately had a huge impact on the team and the Flames' fortunes, playing in 75 games during his **rookie** season. He racked up an impressive list of statistics in the 2013–2014 season, scoring 22 goals to go with 12 assists.

Jiri Hudler

Jiri Hudler came to Calgary in 2012, after seven seasons with the Detroit Red Wings. Although Hudler is still figuring out his role with the Flames, he has already established himself as an offensive weapon in Calgary. In the 2013–2014 season, Hudler appeared in 75 games, scoring 17 goals and collecting a total of 54 points. Hudler knows what it takes to succeed on hockey's grandest stage, as he hoisted the Stanley Cup in Detroit in 2008. The Flames organization hopes he can put that postseason experience and veteran leadership to use in Calgary.

Position: Center
NHL Seasons: 11 (2003–Present)
Born: January 4, 1984, in Olomouc, Czech Republic

All-Time Records

1,219
Most Games Played by a Flame
Jarome Iginla set a number of Flames records, including games played, which underlines his consistency and reliability.

525
Most Career Goals by a Flame
Jarome Iginla dominates this category as well, dwarfing the other top Flames goal scorers.

609
Most Team Career Assists
Al MacInnis was the ultimate teammate and as proof, he has 39 more assists than the second-place player on this list.

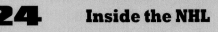

91.3
Highest Team Career Save Percentage

Miikka Kiprusoff is the Flames' leading goaltender in numerous categories. Kiprusoff played hundreds of games in the Flames net, making his save percentage of more than 90 percent an impressive accomplishment.

2,405
Most Career Penalty Minutes by a Flame

Tim Hunter was a famously aggressive player. He was what is known as an "enforcer," who would lay big hits on the opposition.

Timeline

Throughout the team's history, the Calgary Flames have had many memorable events that have become defining moments for the team and its fans.

1980

A group of Calgary businessmen and entrepreneurs acquire the rights to the Atlanta Flames for $16 million. They move the team to their hometown of Calgary, which is hungry for professional hockey.

In 1984, the Flames begin a highly successful run that would last until the end of the 1990–1991 season. In all but one of those six seasons, the Flames would tally at least 90 points per year, reaching the Stanley Cup Final twice during that period.

| 1980 | 1981 | 1982 | 1983 | 1984 | 1985 |

1983

The Flames move into their new home, the Olympic Saddledome, now the Scotiabank Saddledome. It is a world-class arena, built to house the 1988 Winter Olympics. Known for its unique saddle-shaped roof and luxurious amenities, the Saddledome answers Flames fans' requests for a swank new home.

1981

The Flames put together a regular-season record of 39-27-14, which is good enough to punch their ticket to the postseason. The Flames advance to the semifinals, beating the Chicago Blackhawks and the Philadelphia Flyers. Unfortunately, they lose to the Minnesota North Stars in six games.

1989

The Flames win their first and only Stanley Cup, defeating the Montreal Canadiens in six games. It is an emotional ride for the Flames as it is the last season for Lanny McDonald, one of the greatest players in Flames history. In storybook form, McDonald scores a key goal in Game 6 of the final that puts the Flames ahead for good.

The Flames go on a magical run all the way to the Stanley Cup Final. The Flames are the first Canadian team in the final in 10 years, but they drop Game 6 in heartbreaking fashion and are eliminated.

The Future

Hartley's vision for the Flames' future has yet to materialize into wins, but given another season or two, he may be able to follow through on his promise. The fan base in Calgary is as eager as ever, and is always in constant support of its beloved team. Fans are hungry to return to the unstoppable glory days of the Flames, which, hopefully, lie ahead.

1990   **1995**   **2000**   **2005**   **2010**   **2015**

1996

The Flames find their new beacon of hope in an 18-year-old rookie named Jarome Iginla. He makes his debut in the first round of the Stanley Cup, scoring his first NHL point in his first game, and his first NHL goal in his second.

2012

Bob Hartley is brought in as head coach of the team, helping to create an air of change within the Flames organization. Hartley preaches that a new era for the team is just beginning, and starts overhauling the players and staff.

Write a Biography

Life Story

A person's life story can be the subject of a book. This kind of book is called a biography. Biographies often describe the lives of people who have achieved great success. These people may be alive today, or they may have lived many years ago. Reading a biography can help you learn more about a great person.

Get the Facts

Use this book, and research in the library and on the internet, to find out more about your favorite Flame. Learn as much about this player as you can. What position does he play? What are his statistics in important categories? Has he set any records? Also, be sure to write down key events in the person's life. What was his childhood like? What has he accomplished off the field? Is there anything else that makes this person special or unusual?

Use the Concept Web

A concept web is a useful research tool. Read the questions in the concept web on the following page. Answer the questions in your notebook. Your answers will help you write a biography.

Concept Web

Adulthood
- Where does this individual currently reside?
- Does he or she have a family?

Your Opinion
- What did you learn from the books you read in your research?
- Would you suggest these books to others?
- Was anything missing from these books?

Childhood
- Where and when was this person born?
- Describe his or her parents, siblings, and friends.
- Did this person grow up in unusual circumstances?

Write a Biography

Accomplishments off the Field
- What is this person's life's work?
- Has he or she received awards or recognition for accomplishments?
- How have this person's accomplishments served others?

Help and Obstacles
- Did this individual have a positive attitude?
- Did he or she receive help from others?
- Did this person have a mentor?
- Did this person face any hardships?
- If so, how were the hardships overcome?

Accomplishments on the Field
- What records does this person hold?
- What key games and plays have defined his career?
- What are his stats in categories important to his position?

Work and Preparation
- What was this person's education?
- What was his or her work experience?
- How does this person work?
- What is the process he or she uses?

Trivia Time

Take this quiz to test your knowledge of the Calgary Flames. The answers are printed upside down under each question.

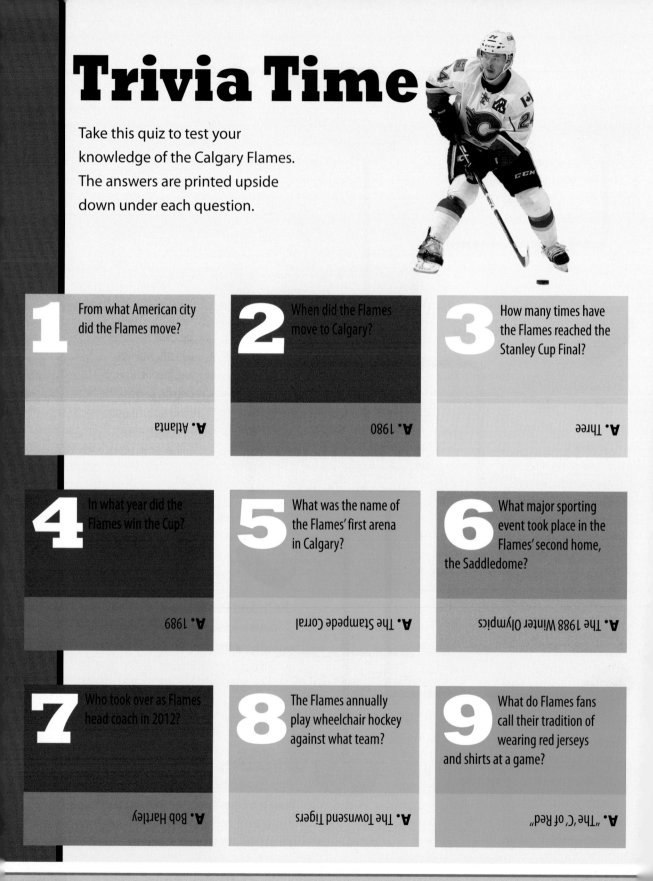

1 From what American city did the Flames move?

A. Atlanta

2 When did the Flames move to Calgary?

A. 1980

3 How many times have the Flames reached the Stanley Cup Final?

A. Three

4 In what year did the Flames win the Cup?

A. 1989

5 What was the name of the Flames' first arena in Calgary?

A. The Stampede Corral

6 What major sporting event took place in the Flames' second home, the Saddledome?

A. The 1988 Winter Olympics

7 Who took over as Flames head coach in 2012?

A. Bob Hartley

8 The Flames annually play wheelchair hockey against what team?

A. The Townsend Tigers

9 What do Flames fans call their tradition of wearing red jerseys and shirts at a game?

A. "The 'C' of Red"

Key Words

assists: a statistic that is attributed to up to two players of the scoring team who shoot, pass, or deflect the puck toward the scoring teammate

entry draft: an annual meeting where different teams in the NHL are allowed to pick new, young players who can join their teams

franchise: a team that is a member of a professional sports league

logo: a symbol that stands for a team or organization

playoff games: a series of games that occur after regular season play

rookie: a player age 26 or younger who has played no more than 25 games in a previous season, nor six or more games in two previous seasons

save percentage: the rate at which a goalie stops shots being made toward his net by the opposing team

Index

1988 Winter Olympics 9, 26, 30

Atlanta Flames 4, 7, 26

"C" of Red, The 19, 30
Cowtown 7
Crisp, Terry 17

Gaudreau, Johnny 4
Giordano, Mark 7, 22

Hartley, Bob 5, 16, 17, 27, 30
helmet 14, 15
Hudler, Jiri 23
Hunter, Tim 25

Iginla, Jarome 20, 22, 24, 27

Kiprusoff, Miikka 25

logo 13, 15, 31

MacInnis, Al 21, 24
McDonald, Lanny 6, 20, 27
Monahan, Sean 22

Olympic Saddledome 9, 26

Scotiabank Saddledome 5, 8, 9, 10, 11, 26
Stampede Corral 7, 30
Sutter, Darryl 17

Townsend Tigers 19, 30

uniform 12, 13, 15

Vernon, Mike 6, 21

Wheelchair Hockey Challenge 19

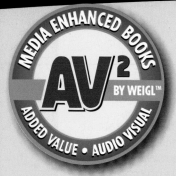

Log on to www.av2books.com

AV² by Weigl brings you media enhanced books that support active learning. Go to www.av2books.com, and enter the special code found on page 2 of this book. You will gain access to enriched and enhanced content that supplements and complements this book. Content includes video, audio, weblinks, quizzes, a slide show, and activities.

AV² Online Navigation

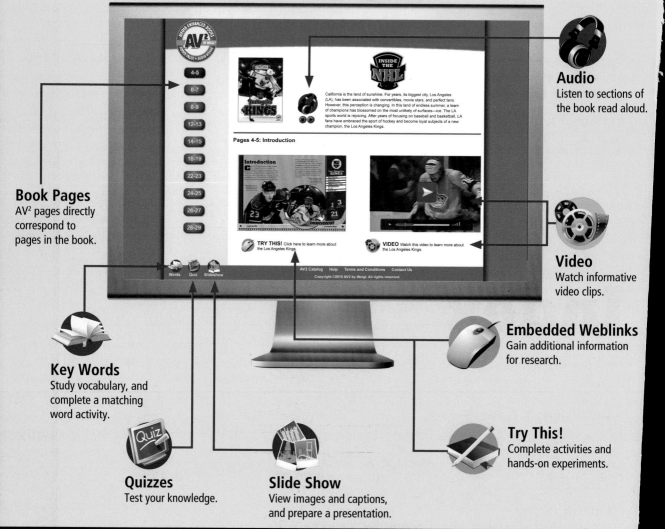

Book Pages
AV² pages directly correspond to pages in the book.

Audio
Listen to sections of the book read aloud.

Video
Watch informative video clips.

Embedded Weblinks
Gain additional information for research.

Key Words
Study vocabulary, and complete a matching word activity.

Quizzes
Test your knowledge.

Slide Show
View images and captions, and prepare a presentation.

Try This!
Complete activities and hands-on experiments.

AV² was built to bridge the gap between print and digital. We encourage you to tell us what you like and what you want to see in the future.

Sign up to be an AV² Ambassador at www.av2books.com/ambassador.

Due to the dynamic nature of the Internet, some of the URLs and activities provided as part of AV² by Weigl may have changed or ceased to exist. AV² by Weigl accepts no responsibility for any such changes. All media enhanced books are regularly monitored to update addresses and sites in a timely manner. Contact AV² by Weigl at 1-866-649-3445 or av2books@weigl.com with any questions, comments, or feedback.